Cambridge **Discovery Education**™

▶ **INTERACTIVE READERS**

Series editor: Bob Hastings

WEIRD ANIMALS

A2

Genevieve Kocienda

CAMBRIDGE
UNIVERSITY PRESS

Discovery
EDUCATION™

CAMBRIDGE UNIVERSITY PRESS
Cambridge, New York, Melbourne, Madrid, Cape Town,
Singapore, São Paulo, Delhi, Mexico City

Cambridge University Press
32 Avenue of the Americas, New York, NY 10013-2473, USA

www.cambridge.org
Information on this title: www.cambridge.org/9781107656642

First published 2014

Printed in Hong Kong, China, by Golden Cup Printing Company Limited

A catalog record for this publication is available from the British Library.

Library of Congress Cataloging-in-Publication Data

Kocienda, G.
  Weird animals / Genevieve Kocienda.
     pages cm. -- (Cambridge discovery interactive readers)
  ISBN 978-1-107-65664-2 (pbk. : alk. paper)
  1. Exotic animals--Juvenile literature. 2. English language--Textbooks for foreign speakers.
  3. Readers (Elementary) I. Title.

SF997.5.E95K64 2013
591.6'2--dc23

                                   2013025124

ISBN 978-1-107-65664-2

Additional resources for this publication at www.cambridge.org

Layout services, art direction, book design, and photo research: Q2ABillSMITH GROUP
Editorial services: Hyphen S.A.
Audio production: CityVox, New York
Video production: Q2ABillSMITH GROUP

Contents

Before You Read:
Get Ready!

Animals are wonderful and there are so many different kinds! Scientists think that there are 8.7 million different kinds of animals on Earth.

Words to Know

Read the information about animals. Then complete the sentences below with the correct highlighted words.

Animals have many different ways of finding a mate. For some birds, the male builds a beautiful nest to attract a female.

Some animals are predators and other animals are prey. The predator wants to eat and kill its prey. That's why some animals have camouflage. It makes it difficult for predators to see them.

1 A _____ animal cannot make eggs or have babies.

2 A _____ animal can make eggs and have babies.

3 _____ makes an animal difficult to see.

4 A _____ is one of a pair of animals that have babies together.

5 An animal that another animal wants to eat is called its _____ .

6 A _____ is an animal that wants to eat another animal.

Birds build a nest for their babies.

Frogs use camouflage to hide from predators.

Video Quest

That's Big!

Watch this video to learn about an animal that lives in the Amazon. Why is it weird?

Words to Know

Read the definitions. Then complete the paragraph with the correct words.

hide: put yourself in a place or do something so that you can't be seen

venom: something that an animal makes that can hurt or kill

survive: live, especially in a difficult place

adaptations: changes that make it easier for an animal to live

environment: the air, water, and land where an animal or plant lives

 For many animals the world is full of dangerous predators, and it isn't easy to **❶** _____. So some animals have weird **❷** _____ that help them to live in their **❸** _____. For example, they may look like something else, a leaf or a rock. This way, they can **❹** _____ from other animals. And some animals, like snakes, are dangerous. They have **❺** _____ in their mouths. When another animal comes near them, they bite!

Snakes bite their prey, and some use venom to kill it.

Skunks have an unusual adaptation.

5

CHAPTER 1

What's So Weird About That?

A warthog

THE WAY AN ANIMAL LOOKS OR BEHAVES MIGHT BE WEIRD TO US, BUT IT WORKS FOR THEM!

Let's look at the warthog. To our eyes, it looks very **weird**! But to another warthog, this animal looks normal, maybe even beautiful. Maybe warthogs think people look weird.

But some animals also look strange to other animals. This helps them survive. For example, some scientists believe that a zebra's stripes are not for camouflage but to make an optical illusion.[1] When a lion sees a group of zebras, it can't see where one zebra ends and another begins. It doesn't know where to bite. So, a zebra's stripes help it to survive.

[1] **optical illusion:** something that looks different from what it really is

Zebras have black and white stripes.

Penguin mates

Sometimes animal **behavior** seems very strange to us, but it's normal in the animal's world.

When some kinds of male penguins want to find a mate, for example, they look for just the right female. This is not easy because penguins sometimes live in groups of thousands. When he finally finds the "girl of his dreams," he doesn't do a dance or sing like other birds. He looks for rocks! He picks up a rock and puts it at the feet of the female he wants to be his mate. If the female takes the rock and puts it in the **nest**, it means she wants him as her mate. The rock is like a wedding ring!

The leafy seadragon looks like seaweed.

CHAPTER 2

Look at That!

ANIMALS HAVE STRANGE ADAPTATIONS TO HIDE FROM PREDATORS, TO FIND PREY TO EAT, OR TO FIND A MATE.

Some animals don't look like animals. They look like part of the environment around them. Camouflage is a good way to hide from predators and survive.

One animal with amazing camouflage is the leafy seadragon, which lives in the waters near Australia. The leafy seadragon is an animal that hides by moving. When it moves through the water, it looks like a piece of seaweed. This is good because its environment has a lot of seaweed! The leafy seadragon's body is green, orange, and gold, and it has small pieces on its body that look just like seaweed. What is the only thing that shows it's an animal? Its eyes!

Leafy seadragons also **behave** in a weird way. The male carries the eggs! After the female **lays** from 100 to 250 eggs, the male picks them up and carries them in a special place under its **tail**. It keeps them for four to six weeks until the eggs hatch and the babies come out.

And leafy seadragons don't have teeth or a stomach. To eat, they suck[2] very small animals into their long mouths. What a weird and wonderful animal!

Another animal with great camouflage is the walking stick. A walking stick is an insect that looks like a stick that can walk. Walking sticks go out at night. During the day, they hide in plants and do not move. Look at the picture. Can a predator see this walking stick? Probably not.

[2]**suck:** pull something into the mouth by taking in air

A walking stick has great camouflage.

A snake caterpillar

The leaf-tailed gecko is a lizard.

Some insects look like other animals. When the snake caterpillar sees a predator, it puts its legs under its body, and makes the front of its body bigger. Then it looks just like a snake! Predators want a delicious[3] caterpillar, but they see a snake and stay away.

There are many insects that look like flowers and plants, but some reptiles do, too. One example is the leaf-tailed gecko. It's a kind of small lizard that lives in Madagascar. When a predator looks for its lunch and sees this gecko, it thinks it's just an old, brown leaf and goes to look somewhere else.

[3]**delicious:** good to eat

Video Quest

Don't Touch!

Watch this video to learn more about two animals that have something on their bodies. What do they have?

Some animals use venom to keep predators away. The saddleback caterpillar of eastern North America looks like a leaf, but it also has **sharp** hairs with venom on them. When a predator touches these hairs, it gets hurt!

A saddleback caterpillar

The blanket octopus doesn't have anything on its own body to keep it safe. It takes something from another very dangerous animal – the Portuguese man-of-war. This animal has tentacles with venom on them. The venom can make animals and people very sick, but it doesn't hurt the blanket octopus. So, when the blanket octopus swims by a Portuguese man-of-war, it takes a tentacle. Then it can hit its predators with the tentacle. That's a very smart octopus!

A blanket octopus

A Portuguese man-of-war has dangerous tentacles.

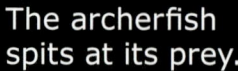

The archerfish
spits at its prey.

Some predators have very
strange adaptations for getting
prey.

The archerfish lives in warm
water all over the world. It looks
normal, like a fish you might have
in your home aquarium.[4] But the
way it gets its prey is weird.

The archerfish eats small insects.
When it looks up and sees an
insect on a leaf near the top of the
water, it spits water at it from its
mouth. The spit hits the insect, the
insect falls into the water, and the
archerfish gets lunch!

[4]**aquarium:** a glass box filled with water that fish live in

A mantis shrimp   A short-tailed shrew

The mantis shrimp of North America must get close to its prey. But when it does, watch out! The mantis shrimp has the fastest arm in the animal kingdom. It moves at 80 kilometers per hour. It hits so hard, it can break the glass in an aquarium! Its prey doesn't know what hit it!

Sometimes an animal looks very sweet and not dangerous at all. But looks don't always tell the whole story.

Look at the short-tailed shrew. It's very small and soft, with little eyes and ears. But it is a dangerous predator. In its mouth are 32 very sharp teeth. And this shrew is one of the few **mammals** with venom. When it **bites** its prey – a mouse, bird, or insect – the venom kills it. The venom is so strong that it can hurt, but not kill, a person.

The short-tailed shrew has to be a good predator. It needs to eat a lot – two or three times its body weight every day!

13

Now let's move away from danger and talk about love!

The male bowerbird of Australia and New Guinea really works hard to get a mate. The males build nests, called bowers. These can be very big and can look like a house. They decorate[5] them with flowers, leaves, vegetables, rocks, insects, and even man-made things, like colored plastic bottle tops. And it's all to get the female to be his mate.

Another hard-working lover is the small manakin bird from South America. It dances up and down tree branches and sings with its wings to show the female it's the best male manakin in the forest! It can hit its wings together 107 times a second to make a *tick, tick, tick* sound. The females love it!

[5]**decorate:** use things to make a place pretty

A male manakin

The female
anglerfish

?

ANALYZE

What things do
different male
animals do to find
mates?

Some animals don't want to dance, sing, build a
beautiful house, or do anything special to get a mate.
Some animals do nothing at all.

For example, there is the anglerfish, which lives in
the Atlantic and Antarctic oceans. The female anglerfish
has a fishing pole on her head. This is a very useful
adaptation for catching food. The male anglerfish,
which is much smaller than the female, doesn't have
this fishing pole. But he doesn't need it – he lets the
female do his fishing.

When a male anglerfish sees a female, he holds on to
her with his sharp teeth. Over time, the male becomes
a part of the female. He loses his eyes and most of
his internal organs.[6] A female can have six or more
"husbands" on her body!

[6]**internal organs:** all the parts inside of your body

A pink handfish

Some animals are weird because of the way they get from one place to another.

Take a look at the pink handfish of Tasmania. The name tells you a lot about this strange animal. First of all, it's pink. But what makes it really weird is its hands. Yes, hands! The pink handfish does not swim around the ocean using fins.[7] It walks along the ocean floor on its hands. What must the other fish think about that?

[7] **fins:** the parts of a fish that it uses to swim

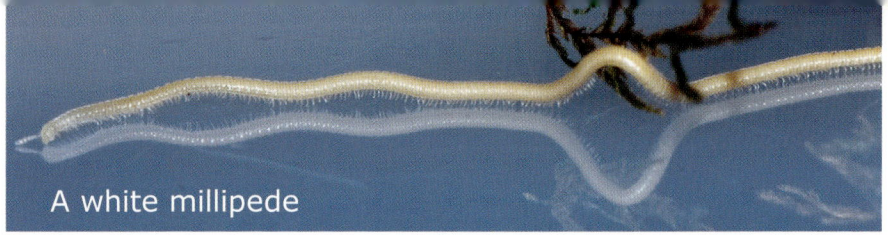

A white millipede

And what about legs? Of course, most animals have legs, but no other animal has as many as *Illacme plenipes*. That's the Latin name for a type of insect, a white millipede, that was found in 2012. So how many legs does it have? 750! That makes it the "leggiest" animal in the world.

Another weird thing about this millipede is that it is found only in one very small place in northern California, USA, but its next closest animal **relative** lives about 16,000 kilometers away in South Africa! What happened? A family argument? Nobody knows.

Some animals have feet and legs, but don't move much. The three-toed sloth lives in Central and South America. It is the slowest mammal on Earth. It moves so little that algae[8] grow on its fur. This makes the fur a little green, and gives the sloth camouflage in the trees. Sloths sleep in trees for 15 to 20 hours a day. They even have their babies in trees! But they come down from the trees about once a week to "go to the bathroom."

[8] **algae:** very, very small, green animals that usually grow on rocks or old trees

Video Quest

That's slow!

Watch this video to learn more about sloths. What is strange about how they live every day?

An okapi　A giraffe

Look at the okapi. It looks like a kind of horse or zebra, but it's not **related** to either of them. Its only animal relative is the giraffe! That's weird because the okapi's neck is not as long as a giraffe's. However, it does have a long tongue that it uses like a hand – just like a giraffe. Scientists didn't know about the okapi until 1900. We still don't know much about the okapi because it lives in the thick forests of central Africa.

The blobfish is really weird. It's the sloth of the sea. It doesn't swim. It floats in the ocean near Tasmania and Australia. It doesn't try to catch food, it just eats anything that comes near its mouth. And it looks completely miserable.[9]

A blobfish

....
[9]**miserable:** very sad

18

bill of
a duck

feet of
a duck

fur of
an otter

tail of
a beaver

A platypus

The platypus of Eastern Australia is maybe the weirdest animal on Earth. It has the tail of a beaver, the fur of an otter, the bill and feet of a duck, and the venom of a snake.

The male platypus has sharp parts on its back feet, called stingers. The stingers have venom. The platypus can hit a predator with its feet and then get away. When the platypus wants to eat, it goes under the water and uses its bill to feel around for insects and small sea life. It also picks up some small rocks in its mouth. The platypus doesn't have teeth, so it uses the rocks to help it "chew" the food.

But the weirdest thing about the platypus is that it's a mammal, but it lays eggs. Wow! That's weird!

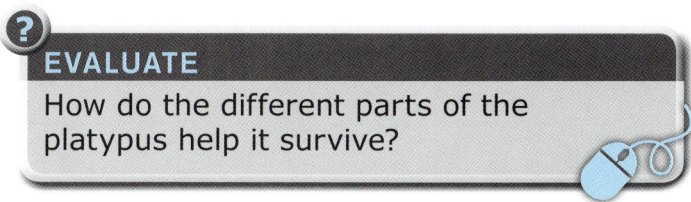

?

EVALUATE

How do the different parts of the platypus help it survive?

A liger

CHAPTER 3

What Do You Think?

THERE ARE MANY WEIRD ANIMALS IN THE WORLD, AND SCIENTISTS ARE MAKING MORE.

What's a *liger*? It's a baby of a tiger mother and a lion father. And a *tigon*? That's a baby of a tiger father and a lion mother. One weird thing about these animals is that the liger is bigger and stronger than its parents, but the tigon is smaller than its parents. Ligers or tigons don't naturally happen in the wild, but sometimes people let tigers and lions have babies in zoos or other places. Many people don't like this, because baby tigons and ligers are often sick.

Do you think it's a good idea for scientists to make hybrids – animals with parents of different species?[10] Is it dangerous for us? Is it bad for the animals?

In many stories and movies, there are hybrid animals, for example, horses with the wings of a bird. Think about the animals from this book or others that you know about. Is there a different species that you would like to make?

What do you think is the "perfect" hybrid animal? What different animal parts does it have?

Scientists are finding new animal species every year. Maybe your "perfect" animal already exists![11] It could be, because the animal world is weird and wonderful!

....

[10] **species:** one kind of animal
[11] **exist:** live

A lion mother with her tigon babies.

? ANALYZE

Why do some scientists want to make hybrids?

21

After You Read

Read the questions and choose Ⓐ, Ⓑ, or Ⓒ.

1 Why do animals have camouflage?

Ⓐ to hide
Ⓑ to run fast
Ⓒ to look for food

2 What animal uses camouflage?

Ⓐ the blobfish
Ⓑ the liger
Ⓒ the leafy seadragon

3 The saddleback caterpillar uses camouflage and what else?

Ⓐ tentacles
Ⓑ sharp teeth
Ⓒ venom

4 Which animal has venom?

Ⓐ the mantis shrimp
Ⓑ the short-tailed shrew
Ⓒ the anglerfish

5 What does the male bowerbird do that is special?

Ⓐ It dances.
Ⓑ It decorates a nest.
Ⓒ It gives a rock to its mate.

6 Which animal looks like parts of a few other animals?

Ⓐ the short-tailed shrew
Ⓑ the three-toed sloth
Ⓒ the platypus

Complete the Sentences

Use the words in the box to complete the sentences.

> female   male   mate   predators   prey

1 Some birds sing songs to find a _____.

2 The _____ leafy seadragon carries the eggs. That's very strange in the animal world.

3 Most _____ are faster than the animals they eat.

4 _____ penguins lay only one egg.

5 Smaller animals are usually _____ for bigger animals.

Complete the Text

Use the words in the box to complete the paragraphs.

> adaptations   camouflage   hide   predators   venom

Many animals use **1** _____ to keep safe. If their **2** _____ can't see them, then they can't eat them. Some animals look so much like their environment they can **3** _____ right in front of you!

And some animals have two different **4** _____ to keep safe. Camouflage and a dangerous **5** _____ that can hurt the other animal!

23

Answer Key

Words to Know, page 4

1 male **2** female **3** Camouflage **4** mate **5** prey
6 predator

Words to Know, page 5

1 survive **2** adaptations **3** environment **4** hide **5** venom

Video Quest, page 5

It is unusually large. It is an herbivore.

Video Quest, page 10

They have sharp quills to protect them.

Analyze, page 15

Some sing, some dance, some decorate a nest.

Video Quest, page 17

It spends 99 percent of its life upside down in a tree.

Evaluate, page 19

Its bill helps it get food, its feet help it swim, its fur keeps
it warm, its venom helps it survive against predators.

Analyze, page 21   *Answers will vary.*

Choose the Correct Answers, page 22

1 A **2** C **3** C **4** B **5** B **6** C

Complete the Sentences, page 23

1 mate **2** male **3** predators **4** Female **5** prey

Complete the Text, page 23

1 camouflage **2** predators **3** hide **4** adaptations
5 venom